How to Write an Essay

by Cecilia Minden
and Kate Roth

CHERRY LAKE PUBLISHING · ANN ARBOR, MICHIGAN

Published in the United States of America by Cherry Lake Publishing
Ann Arbor, Michigan
www.cherrylakepublishing.com

Content Adviser: Gail Dickinson, PhD, Associate Professor, Old Dominion University, Norfolk, Virginia

Photo Credits: Page 4, ©Khakimullin Aleksandr/Shutterstock, Inc.; page 6, ©iStockphoto.com/kali9; page 10, ©Monkey Business Images/Shutterstock, Inc.; page 13, ©iofoto/Shutterstock, Inc.; page 14, ©wavebreakmedia ltd/Shutterstock, Inc.; page 16, ©Juriah Mosin/Shutterstock, Inc.; page 18, ©iStockphoto.com/gbh007; page 21, ©sonya etchison/Shutterstock, Inc.

Library of Congress Cataloging-in-Publication Data
Minden, Cecilia.
  How to write an essay / by Cecilia Minden and Kate Roth.
       p. cm. — (Language arts explorer junior)
  Includes bibliographical references and index.
  ISBN 978-1-61080-492-9 (lib. bdg.) —
ISBN 978-1-61080-579-7 (e-book) — ISBN 978-1-61080-666-4 (pbk.)
1. English language—Composition and exercises—Study and teaching (Elementary)—Juvenile literature. 2. Essay—Authorship—Problems, exercises, etc.—Juvenile literature. I. Roth, Kate. II. Title.
  LB1576.M5344 2012
  372.62'3—dc23   2012008924

Cherry Lake Publishing would like to acknowledge the work of The Partnership for 21st Century Skills. Please visit www.21stcenturyskills.org for more information.

Printed in the United States of America
Corporate Graphics Inc.
July 2012
CLFA11

Table of Contents

CHAPTER ONE

Sharing Your Opinion

Do you and your friends ever discuss your opinions about movies?

What do you think? You've probably heard that question before. Someone asked for your thoughts or **opinion**. Maybe it was about a book or a movie. Sometimes an opinion is about an **issue**. How can you share your ideas with others? You might give a speech or start a Web site. You can also write an **essay**.

An essay consists of three parts:

- State your opinion or ideas in the **introduction**.
- Support your opinion or ideas in the **body**.
- Summarize your opinion or ideas in the **conclusion**.

Here is what you will need to complete the activities in this book:

- Blank notebook paper
- Pencil with an eraser
- A computer (optional)

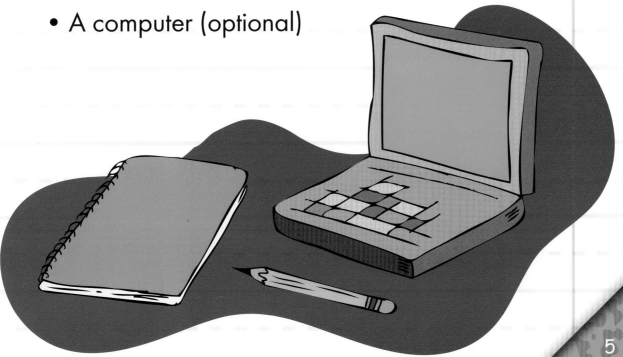

CHAPTER TWO

What Do You Think?

Have you ever helped your parents cook dinner?

Essays are always written in the first person **perspective**. This means that your own thoughts and voice, as the author, must come through to the reader. These are *your* ideas about an **event** or an issue.

For example, you could write an essay about the time you helped to cook dinner. You learned that vegetables taste great when you helped cook. An essay about an issue can explain your opinion about something. For example, maybe you think the local newspaper should have a section just for kids. Maybe you think your parents should raise your allowance. Make a list of ideas and choose one for your essay.

Once you've selected your topic, think of ideas you have related to that subject.

Writing is done in one of three different perspectives. Each one represents a different point of view. Essays are written in the first person, but you will use the other perspectives for different projects.

- FIRST PERSON: the writer's thoughts
  I think vegetables taste great!
- SECOND PERSON: the reader's thoughts
  You think vegetables taste great!
- THIRD PERSON: another person's thoughts
  He thinks vegetables taste great!

To get a copy of this activity, visit www.cherrylakepublishing.com/activities.

ACTIVITY

Choose a Topic

In this activity you will make a list of possible topics for your essay and take notes on your idea.

INSTRUCTIONS:

1. Write down a list of possible topics for your essay.
2. Think about events or issues about which you have an opinion.
3. Choose one for the topic of your essay.
4. Write a sentence explaining your overall opinion of your chosen topic.
5. Make a list of at least three points to support your opinion.

Sample Topic List

TOPIC IDEAS
- (Vegetables taste better when I help cook them.)
- The library needs more science fiction books.
- The newspaper needs a kids' section.
- I deserve a bigger allowance.

Sample List of Opinion and Thoughts

OPINION AND THOUGHTS ABOUT YOUR TOPIC

Vegetables:

My opinion is that they taste better when I help to cook them.

1. I do not really like vegetables.
2. I got to buy them and help cook them.
3. They tasted really good.

CHAPTER THREE

Write Your Introduction

Begin your essay with an introduction to get the reader's attention. The introduction will contain several sentences. The first sentence might be a question or a fact. For example, an essay about learning to like vegetables might begin with "I used to think carrots tasted gross." It could also begin with "Do you think carrots taste

Sometimes food just tastes better if you cook it yourself!

gross?" The introduction also includes the topic sentence. The topic sentence explains the main topic. For example, "Then I learned how to cook my own vegetables, and now they taste pretty good!"

ACTIVITY

Introduction and Topic Sentence

In this activity you will write the first paragraph for your essay.

INSTRUCTIONS:
1. Write three possible first sentences to your essay.
2. Pick one that will make your readers most interested in reading your essay.
3. Add at least two more sentences to your introductory paragraph. These sentences should get your readers interested in your topic and state your opinion.

Activity continued on page 12

Activity continued from page 11.

Sample Topic Sentence

Ideas for First Sentence:

1. I want to eat healthy, but I think it is really hard!
2. I used to think carrots tasted gross.
3. Grown-ups always say, "Eat your vegetables!"

Sample Introduction

I used to think carrots tasted gross. I also did not like broccoli or cauliflower or most other vegetables. Then I learned how to cook my own vegetables, and now they taste pretty good! It is easy to be healthy when you help in the kitchen.

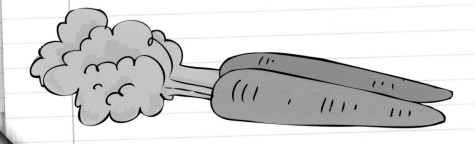

CHAPTER FOUR

Write Your Ideas

Include a lot of details to make your essay more interesting for the reader.

The body of the essay comes after the introduction. How will you help the reader understand why the ideas in your topic sentence are important to you? Refer to your notes. What ideas did you write to support the topic? Write a few sentences about each of those ideas. For example, you are writing about how you have learned that vegetables can taste good. Write about the time you learned to like vegetables after buying and cooking them with your mom or dad. Help the reader experience each of those things with you. Use **adjectives** to make the writing more alive. Let the reader experience the event through your eyes.

If you have a computer, you can type your essay instead of writing it out by hand.

To get a copy of this activity, visit www.cherrylakepublishing.com/activities.

ACTIVITY

The Body

In this activity you will write the main paragraph of your essay.

INSTRUCTIONS:
1. Look at your notes on your topic.
2. Write a sentence for each of your ideas.
3. Put the sentences into a paragraph.
4. Use adjectives to make the paragraph come alive for the reader.
5. Write using the first person perspective.

Essays can be funny, serious, or a little of both.

Sample Body

One day, my dad got tired of hearing me complain about eating vegetables. He decided I should learn how to cook them myself. We went to the market. Dad gave me money to buy my own vegetables. It was fun to see all the colors and shapes. I picked out ones that looked fresh and bright. Maybe vegetables weren't so bad after all. When we got home, we made vegetable lasagna. It was fun, and, with Dad's help, I used a real knife to cut up the vegetables. Then I filled a pan with pasta, cheese, and vegetables. We watched it bubble in the oven. It smelled delicious. When I served dinner to my family, I felt proud. I also cleaned my plate of every single bite of vegetables.

CHAPTER FIVE

Write Your Conclusion

A good conclusion will make the reader think hard about everything he or she has just read.

End your essay with a summary of your ideas. Restate the main ideas of your essay. This helps the reader remember what you have said. You might choose a **quotation** or fact that leaves the reader thinking about something.

To get a copy of this activity, visit www.cherrylakepublishing.com/activities.

ACTIVITY

Summary and Conclusion

In this activity you will finish your essay.

INSTRUCTIONS:
1. Write the final paragraph of your essay.
2. Restate the main idea of your essay.
3. End with a quotation or fact that leaves the reader thinking.

Sample Conclusion

I now like to eat carrots, broccoli, cauliflower, and spinach. I am good at cutting carrots. Try to find new recipes with vegetables to cook. Go ask an adult if you can help go shopping and make dinner together. You may be surprised how yummy vegetables can be!

You may want to illustrate your essay with a picture or drawing.

CHAPTER SIX

Write a Title

An attention-grabbing title will make people want to read your work.

Is your essay complete? Not quite! Take time to reread your essay. Check for grammar or spelling errors. Once the essay is exactly right, give it a title. Try to make the title one that will make the reader curious. Instead of *I Like Vegetables*, your title could be *Yucky to Yummy*. Which one would get your attention?

To get a copy of this activity, visit
www.cherrylakepublishing.com/activities.

ACTIVITY

Final Copy and Title

INSTRUCTIONS:
1. Type your essay or rewrite it in your neatest handwriting.
2. Give your essay a title.
3. You may want to include an illustration.

Yucky to Yummy

I used to think carrots tasted gross. I also did not like broccoli or cauliflower or most other vegetables. Then I learned how to cook my own vegetables, and now they taste pretty good! It is easy to be healthy when you help in the kitchen.

One day, my dad got tired of hearing me complain about eating vegetables. He decided I should learn how to cook them myself. We went to the market. Dad gave me money to buy my own vegetables. It was fun to see all the colors and shapes. I picked out ones that looked fresh and bright. Maybe vegetables weren't so bad after all. When we got home, we made vegetable lasagna. It was fun, and, with Dad's help, I used a real knife to cut up the vegetables. Then I filled a pan with pasta, cheese, and vegetables. We watched it bubble in the oven. It smelled delicious. When I served dinner to my family, I felt proud. I also cleaned my plate of every single bite of vegetables.

I now like to eat carrots, broccoli, cauliflower, and spinach. I am good at cutting carrots. Try to find new recipes with vegetables to cook. Go ask an adult if you can help go shopping and make dinner together. You may be surprised how yummy vegetables can be!

To get a copy of this activity, visit www.cherrylakepublishing.com/activities.

ACTIVITY

Final Changes

Read the instructions carefully. Check everything one more time.

☐ YES ☐ NO Is my essay about my opinion of an event or issue?

☐ YES ☐ NO Does my essay have an introduction, a body, and a conclusion?

☐ YES ☐ NO Is my essay written in the first person perspective?

☐ YES ☐ NO Does my essay begin with a sentence to get the reader's attention?

☐ YES ☐ NO Do I have a summary of my ideas in the conclusion?

☐ YES ☐ NO Does my essay have a good title?

☐ YES ☐ NO Do I use correct grammar and spelling?

Now that you know how to write an essay, you may find that you want to write more. You have opinions on many topics. There are authors who are famous for their essays. Who knows? Maybe one day you will be one of them!

Henry David Thoreau wrote famous essays about his life on Walden Pond.

Try writing an essay about your favorite sport or a hobby you enjoy.

Glossary

adjectives (AD-jik-tivz) words used to describe nouns

body (BAH-dee) the main part of a piece of writing

conclusion (kuhn-KLOO-zhuhn) the end of a piece of writing

essay (ES-ay) a short written work about a particular topic

event (eh-VENT) something of importance that happens

introduction (in-truh-DUHK-shuhn) the beginning of a piece of writing

issue (ISH-oo) a topic for debate or discussion

opinion (uh-PIN-yuhn) personal feelings about a topic

paragraph (PARE-uh-graf) a group of sentences about a certain idea or subject

perspective (pur-SPEK-tiv) a point of view

quotation (kwoh-TAY-shuhn) a sentence or short passage that is written or spoken by one person and repeated by another

For More Information

BOOK

Minden, Cecilia, and Kate Roth. *How to Write About Your Adventure*. Ann Arbor, MI: Cherry Lake Publishing, 2011.

WEB SITES

Enchanted Learning
www.enchantedlearning.com/essay
Check out some good suggestions for essay topics.

International Reading Association—Read Write Think
www.readwritethink.org/classroom-resources/student-interactives essay-30063.html
Use the Essay Map to help you create your essay.

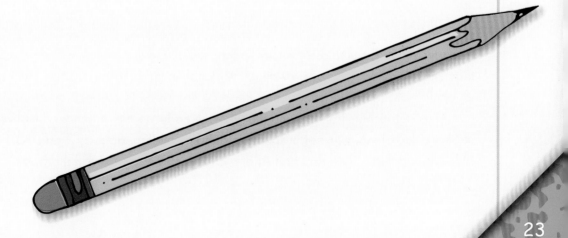

Index

About the Authors

Cecilia Minden, PhD, is the former director of the Language and Literacy Program at Harvard Graduate School of Education. She earned her doctorate from the University of Virginia. While at Harvard, Dr. Minden also taught several writing courses. Her research focused on early literacy skills and developing phonics curricula. She is now an educational consultant and the author of more than 100 books for children. Dr. Minden lives with her family in Chapel Hill, North Carolina. She likes to write early in the morning while the house is still quiet.

Kate Roth has a doctorate from Harvard University in language and literacy and a master's from Columbia University Teachers College in curriculum and teaching. Her work focuses on writing instruction in the primary grades. She has taught first grade, kindergarten, and Reading Recovery. She has also instructed hundreds of teachers from around the world in early literacy practices. She lives in Shanghai, China, with her husband and three children, ages 3, 7, and 10. Her oldest two children, Annabel and Andrew, wrote the essay used in this book.